Biographies

Phillis Wheatley

Colonial American Poet

by Laura Purdie Salas

Consultant:
Dr. Kenneth Goings, Professor and Chair
Department of African American and African Studies
The Ohio State University
Columbus, Ohio

Capstone *press*

Mankato, Minnesota

Fact Finders is published by Capstone Press,
151 Good Counsel Drive, P.O. Box 669, Mankato, Minnesota 56002.
www.capstonepress.com

Library of Congress Cataloging-in-Publication Data
Salas, Laura Purdie.
  Phillis Wheatley : colonial American poet / by Laura Purdie Salas.
  p. cm. — (Fact finders. Biographies)
  Includes bibliographical references and index.
  ISBN-13: 978-0-7368-5435-1 (hardcover)
  ISBN-10: 0-7368-5435-5 (hardcover)
  1. Wheatley, Phillis, 1753–1784—Juvenile literature. 2. Poets, American—Colonial
period, ca. 1600–1775—Biography—Juvenile literature. 3. Slaves—United States—
Biography—Juvenile literature. 4. African American poets—Biography—Juvenile literature.
I. Title. II. Series.
PS866.W5Z6936 2006
811'.1—dc22   2005022579

Summary: An introduction to the life of Phillis Wheatley, the colonial slave who became
one of America's first black poets.

Editorial Credits
Megan Schoeneberger, editor; Juliette Peters, set designer; Linda Clavel and Scott Thoms,
    book designers; Kelly Garvin, photo researcher/photo editor

Photo Credits
Art Resource, NY/Schomburg Center, 1
Bridgeman Art Library/Massachusetts Historical Society, Boston, MA, 10–11
Capstone Press/Bob Lentz, cover, 27
Corbis, 19; Bettmann, 5
Getty Images/Hulton Archive, 18
The Granger Collection, New York, 6–7, 8, 9, 13, 15, 22, 25, 26
Mary Evans Picture Library, 16–17
Photographs and Prints Division, The Schomberg Center for Research in Black Culture, The
    New York Public Library, Astor, Lenox and Tilden Foundation, 21

1 2 3 4 5 6 11 10 09 08 07 06

Table of Contents

Chapter 1

A Test

Phillis Wheatley stood in front of politicians, ministers, poets, and scientists. The group of 18 white men had gathered to find out if Phillis, a teenage **slave**, was really a poet.

Phillis was unlike other slaves. In 1772, most slaves did not receive an education. They could not read or write. But Phillis could. With the help of her owners, she had studied history and geography. She also wrote poetry. Now, her owners wanted to help publish her poetry in a book.

The men, like many whites at that time, didn't believe that black people could write poetry. They quizzed Phillis about poetry, history, and other topics.

Unlike most other slaves, Phillis Wheatley could read and write.

Phillis answered all of their questions, showing her intelligence and creativity. All 18 men then signed a paper to say that they believed she had written the poems. With the support of these men, Phillis could publish the book.

Chapter 2

From Africa to North America

Phillis' early childhood is a mystery. Nobody knows who her parents were or what they named her. Nobody knows for sure where or when she was born. Experts today guess that Phillis was born in West Africa in about 1753.

Phillis' early childhood is unknown because she was a slave. Slave traders kidnapped Phillis in 1761. They took her away from her home and her family. They put her on a slave ship to North America. Nobody wrote down anything about Phillis' past.

Kidnapped Africans were chained together and led to slave markets along the coast of Africa.

The trip to North America was horrible. Aboard the smelly, crowded ship, the captives suffered illness, hunger, and abuse. Some decided they would rather die than become slaves. These people jumped overboard and drowned.

Susanna Wheatley saw an ad similar to this one offering slaves for sale. ▼

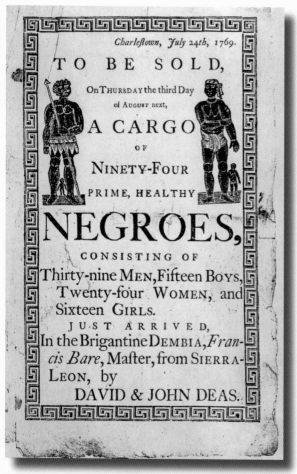

The ship arrived in Boston, Massachusetts, on July 11, 1761. Later that month, ads for the slaves appeared in the Boston paper.

Susanna Wheatley, wife of a local tailor, saw an ad. She wanted someone to help with housework and went to purchase a slave.

Susanna was drawn to the little African girl. The girl wore only a dirty cloth. She had lost her front baby teeth, which meant she was about 8 years old. Susanna and John Wheatley bought the girl and named her after the slave ship, the *Phillis*.

▲ Slaves were often sold at auctions to whomever would pay the highest price.

Kind Owners

Susanna and John treated Phillis kindly. They gave her few chores. While most slaves lived in unheated shacks, Phillis' bedroom was heated. At night, a burning candle lit her room.

The Wheatleys' kindness didn't change the fact that Phillis was a slave. In public, Phillis often could not sit at a table with white people. She had to sit at a separate table.

Chapter 3

Poetry

Phillis was smart and curious. She learned very quickly. The Wheatleys asked their daughter, Mary, to teach Phillis. Phillis studied history, geography, and literature. In time, Phillis was better educated than most people, black or white.

Phillis also learned about religion and politics in the Wheatley home. She became a Christian, like the Wheatleys. She learned that some American **colonists** wanted to be free of British rule.

FACT!

Most slaves were not given an education. Between 1761 and 1784, not a single black child was enrolled in Boston's schools.

By the 1700s, Boston had become an important city in the American colonies.

Writing

Of all her studies, Phillis especially liked poetry. When she was 12, Phillis began writing poems. She wrote **elegies** to honor the lives of people who had died. She also wrote about events going on in the world around her.

On December 21, 1767, the *Newport Mercury* newspaper in Rhode Island printed one of Phillis' poems. "On Messrs Hussey and Coffin" told the story of two men who had been caught in a storm at sea.

QUOTE

"Without any Assistance from School Education, and by only what she was taught in the Family, she, in sixteen Months Time from her Arrival, attained the English language."
—John Wheatley, referring to Phillis in a letter

Phillis wrote "To the University of Cambridge, in New-England" the same year. In the poem, Phillis told the students to be serious about learning.

In 1770, Reverend George Whitefield died. This well-known English minister had visited the Wheatleys. Phillis wrote an elegy called "On the Death of the Rev. Mr. George Whitefield."

Phillis handwrote this copy of her poem "To the University of Cambridge, in New-England." ➡

The poem was first printed in Boston. Then, Phillis sent the poem to a friend of Susanna's, the Countess of Huntingdon, in London. Whitefield had been the Countess' minister. The Countess convinced a London publisher to print the elegy.

Proving Herself

After Phillis' success, Susanna Wheatley wanted to publish a book of Phillis' poems. No American publisher would print it. Too many colonists doubted that a slave could write poetry.

The Countess of Huntingdon helped again. She talked to Archibald Bell, a London publisher. Bell wanted proof of Phillis' writing ability before he would print the book.

In 1772, Phillis met with the governor of Massachusetts and other area leaders. The leaders tested Phillis, and she passed their tests. Bell agreed to publish Phillis' book in London.

The Countess of Huntingdon was a wealthy woman who helped Phillis find someone to publish her book. ➡

Chapter 4

Adventure

Phillis had suffered from asthma for many years. By 1773, Phillis was having difficulty breathing. A doctor suggested that sea air would help.

At the same time, Phillis' book was being prepared in London. The Wheatleys decided that Phillis should sail to London where she could promote her book.

On May 8, 1773, Phillis boarded a ship in Boston. The trip to London was unlike her first ocean voyage. This time, Phillis was not a prisoner. She walked freely on the ship's deck. She wrote poetry and ate as much as she liked.

This illustration shows London in the 1700s, about the time when Phillis visited.

London

The British welcomed Phillis. They admired her poetry and loved her dark skin. They also enjoyed her polite, intelligent conversation.

▲ Benjamin Franklin was one of the people Phillis met while in London.

Phillis met many people in London, including Benjamin Franklin. He was in London to work for colonists' rights. Franklin and other colonists were unhappy with the taxes charged by Great Britain's leaders. They wanted to change the way the British ruled the colonies.

In July, a letter arrived from Boston. Susanna Wheatley was ill. Phillis left London to return to Boston.

Freedom and Grief

Phillis cared for Susanna for seven months. During that time, John Wheatley freed her. Phillis was no longer a slave.

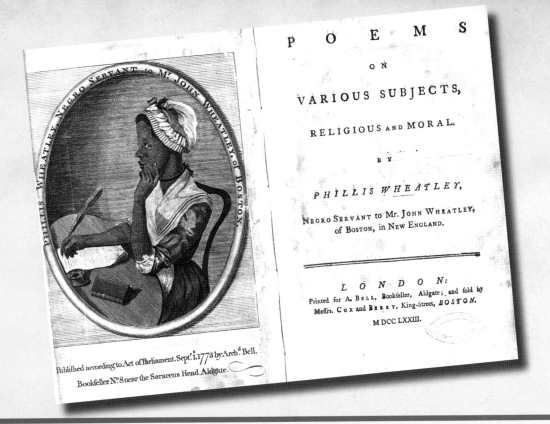

POEMS

ON

VARIOUS SUBJECTS,

RELIGIOUS AND MORAL.

BY

PHILLIS WHEATLEY,

NEGRO SERVANT to Mr. JOHN WHEATLEY,
of BOSTON, in NEW ENGLAND.

LONDON:
Printed for A. BELL, Bookseller, Aldgate; and sold by
Messrs. COX and BERRY, King-Street, BOSTON.
MDCCLXXIII.

▲ A drawing of Phillis appeared in her book.

Phillis' book was published in September 1773. *Poems on Various Subjects, Religious and Moral* was the first published poetry book written in English by a black woman.

In March 1774, Susanna died. In a letter to a friend, Phillis wrote that she felt like she had lost a parent.

Chapter 5

On Her Own

After Susanna's death, Phillis continued to live in the Wheatley home. She helped take care of John Wheatley.

Phillis tried to sell copies of her book. But not many people bought it. The people of Boston were more concerned with freedom from Great Britain than they were with poetry.

The American Revolution

America went to war against Britain in 1775. In October, Phillis wrote a poem called "To His Excellency George Washington." Washington was the commander of the American army. Phillis visited him at his headquarters in 1776.

This portrait of Phillis was drawn when she was 18 years old.

America declared its **independence** in 1776. But the fighting continued. Phillis wrote several poems about the war. Two were "On the Capture of General Lee" and "On the Death of General Wooster." In her poems, she praised America and its fight for freedom.

▲ The opening battle of the Revolutionary War took place in Lexington, Massachusetts in 1775. Many of the battles took place near Boston.

Hard Times

John Wheatley died in March 1778. Phillis was about 25 years old. A month later, she married a free black shopkeeper named John Peters. They had three children together. Two of their small children died from illnesses.

Life was very difficult for Phillis as a free African American. Many white people did not want to hire African Americans. Phillis and her husband struggled. He often left to look for work. Phillis worked as a maid. She also kept writing, but nobody would publish her work.

Chapter 6

Wheatley's Legacy

The American Revolution finally ended in 1783. Phillis wrote a poem about it called "Liberty and Peace." This poem was published in 1784. It was her last published poem.

Phillis' asthma made her weak and ill. She died December 5, 1784. She was only 31 years old. Phillis' last surviving child died of an illness the same day. They were buried together.

A Lasting Voice

In the early 1800s, **abolitionist** publishers kept printing her poetry. These publishers used Phillis' poetry to show that slaves had just as much talent and intelligence as white people.

The statue's inscription reads:

PHILLIS WHEATLEY

CA. 1753–1784

BORN IN WEST AFRICA AND SOLD AS A SLAVE
FROM THE SHIP *PHILLIS* IN COLONIAL BOSTON.
SHE WAS A LITERARY PRODIGY WHOSE 1773 VOLUME
POEMS ON VARIOUS SUBJECTS, RELIGIOUS
AND MORAL WAS THE FIRST BOOK PUBLISHED BY
AN AFRICAN WRITER IN AMERICA

This Boston statue honors Phillis Wheatley and her poetry.

Phillis was one of the first African Americans to publish poetry in the English language. She proved that slaves were as smart and as creative as their masters. Today, many schools and groups are named in her honor.

Phillis died at a young age. But because of her poetry, her voice did not die with her.

Phillis signed this autograph in Boston. ▼

I am very affectionately your Friend
Phillis Wheatley

Boston March 21. 1774.

Fast Facts

Full name: Phillis Wheatley

Birth date: Unknown. Experts believe she was born in about 1753.

Died: December 5, 1784

Parents: Unknown. She was purchased by John and Susanna Wheatley.

Siblings: Unknown. John and Susanna Wheatley had two children, Nathaniel and Mary.

Hometown: Unknown. Experts believe she was born in Senegal or Gambia in West Africa; lived in Boston, Massachusetts.

Religion: Christian

Education: Tutored by the Wheatley family

Major works:
Poems on Various Subjects, Religious and Moral

Time Line

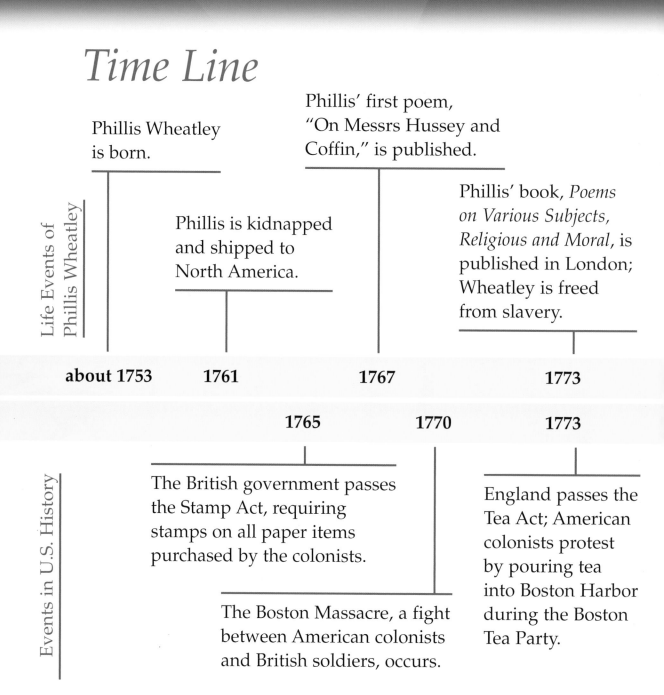

Life Events of Phillis Wheatley

Phillis Wheatley is born.

Phillis is kidnapped and shipped to North America.

Phillis' first poem, "On Messrs Hussey and Coffin," is published.

Phillis' book, *Poems on Various Subjects, Religious and Moral*, is published in London; Wheatley is freed from slavery.

about 1753   **1761**   **1767**   **1773**

1765   **1770**   **1773**

Events in U.S. History

The British government passes the Stamp Act, requiring stamps on all paper items purchased by the colonists.

The Boston Massacre, a fight between American colonists and British soldiers, occurs.

England passes the Tea Act; American colonists protest by pouring tea into Boston Harbor during the Boston Tea Party.

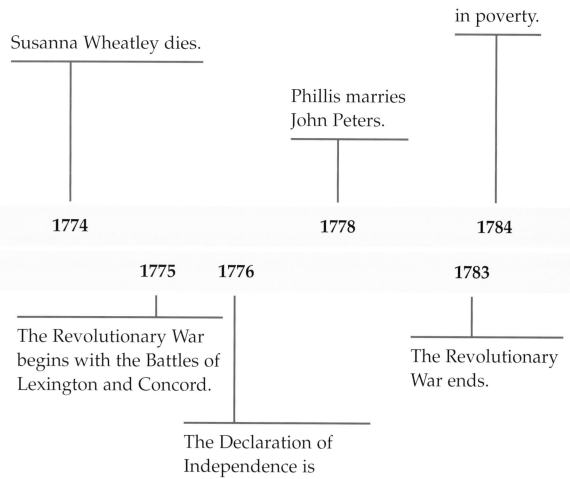

Susanna Wheatley dies.

Phillis dies
in poverty.

Phillis marries
John Peters.

1774

1778

1784

1775   **1776**

1783

The Revolutionary War
begins with the Battles of
Lexington and Concord.

The Revolutionary
War ends.

The Declaration of
Independence is
signed in Philadelphia.

Glossary

abolitionist (ab-uh-LISH-uh-nist)—a person who worked to end slavery before the Civil War

colonist (KOL-uh-nist)—a person who lives in a colony; a colony is land ruled by another country.

elegy (EL-uh-jee)—a poem written in memory of someone who has died

independence (in-di-PEN-duhnss)—freedom from the control of other people or things

slave (SLAYV)—someone who is owned by another person and thought of as property

Internet Sites

FactHound offers a safe, fun way to find Internet sites related to this book.
All of the sites on FactHound have been researched by our staff.

Here's how:

1. Visit *www.facthound.com*
2. Type in this special code **0736854355** for age-appropriate sites. Or enter a search word related to this book for a more general search.
3. Click on the **Fetch It** button.

FactHound will fetch the best sites for you!

Read More

Doak, Robin S. *Phillis Wheatley: Slave and Poet.* Signature Lives. Minneapolis: Compass Point Books, 2006.

Lasky, Kathryn. *A Voice of Her Own: The Story of Phillis Wheatley, Slave Poet.* Cambridge, Mass.: Candlewick Press, 2003.

Roza, Greg. *Guide My Pen: The Poems of Phillis Wheatley.* Great Moments in American History. New York: Rosen, 2004.

Index